MAY YOU ENJOY THIS BOOK

The Public Library is free to everyone living in Nashua. You can increase its usefulness to all by returning books promptly, on or before the "Date Due" as stamped.

If you derive pleasure and profit from the use of your Public Library, why not tell others about its many services

THE NASHUA PUBLIC LIBRARY

Nashua, N.H.

SQUIRREL WATCHING

SQUIRREL WATCHING

by Miriam Schlein

Photographs by Marjorie Pillar

HarperCollins*Publishers*

JUV
599.323
S
Copy 1
NPL

PHOTO CREDITS

Courtesy Department of Library Services, American Museum of
Natural History: p. 12 (left) Neg. No. 107034 (E. H. Baynes); p. 12
(right) Neg. No. 2A 5030; p. 48 (bottom) Neg. No. 19682 (Julius
Kirschner); p. 52 Neg. No. 102850 (Mary C. Dickerson); p. 53 Neg.
No. 122875 (Clyde Fisher); p. 55 Neg. No. 323944 (J. P. Pardoe); p.
57 Neg. No. 335448 (K. Chambers). Copyright © New York Zoo-
logical Society: p. 48 (top). Courtesy City Clerk, Olney, Il: p. 15.

Squirrel Watching
Text copyright © 1992 by Miriam Schlein
Photographs copyright © 1992 by Marjorie Paula Pillar

Typography by Dan O'Leary
1 2 3 4 5 6 7 8 9 10
First Edition

Library of Congress Cataloging-in-Publication Data
Schlein, Miriam.
    Squirrel watching / by Miriam Schlein ; photographs by Marjorie
Pillar.
        p.   cm.
    Summary: Describes the many different kinds of squirrels and their
behavior, including food-gathering, nesting, and the raising of
young.
    ISBN 0-06-022753-2. — ISBN 0-06-022754-0 (lib. bdg.)
    1. Squirrels—Juvenile literature. [1. Squirrels.]   I. Pillar,
Marjorie, ill.   II. Title.
QL737.R68S34   1992   91-6481
599.32′32—dc20   CIP
                                                            AC

Contents

Chapter 1
Squirrel Parachutes

Twelve-year-old Terry was delivering newspapers in Baraboo, Wisconsin, when he happened to look up and see two squirrels chasing each other high in the treetops, almost 100 feet over the street. Then, he says, "to my horror, one of the squirrels fell, making a dull *splut* sound on the asphalt surface below. I tried not to imagine what it must have felt like. But after about fifteen seconds, it suddenly got up, ran to the nearest tree, and scampered up the trunk as though nothing had happened."

A miracle? Not for a squirrel!

Squirrels (opposite) are at home in the city.

Here is another hard-to-believe true squirrel story:

A man living on the fifteenth floor of an apartment building looked out one day and was surprised to see a squirrel sitting on his air conditioner. He didn't know how it got up there. But he saw how it got down. As he watched, fascinated, he saw the squirrel go down floor by floor, jumping and landing on one air conditioner after another, till it reached the ground.

Probably the record leap was made by a squirrel in Mexico. It leaped off a cliff and landed 500 feet below. It didn't seem to be hurt. After landing, it just walked away.

How is that possible?

As a squirrel leaps—or falls—it can make a sort of natural parachute with its body. It spreads out its legs, flattens its body, and stretches out its tail. This catches the air the way a parachute does, and slows the fall.

Look at a squirrel. What's the first thing you notice? The tail! It's long and fuzzy, almost feathery-looking. The squirrel holds it up like a banner.

But the tail does more than look pretty. It's really important to the squirrel. As a squirrel leaps from branch to branch, its tail

Gray squirrel with tail held high

helps it to steer through the air. Held at an angle, the tail creates wind resistance. This helps the squirrel to control its direction (the same way an airplane rudder steers a plane through the air).

Have you ever seen a squirrel running along on a telephone wire, or a fence, or a clothesline? He uses his tail to help keep his balance, holding it out the way a circus tightrope walker uses a balancing pole—the way you hold your arms stretched out to help keep your balance when you're walking on something narrow.

The squirrel even gets its name from its tail. In ancient times a Greek poet named Oppian noticed that on sunny days this little animal would shade itself with its tail. So he gave it the name *skiouros*, a combination of the Greek words *skia* (shade) and *oura* (tail), meaning "shade-tail" or "shadow-tail." In Latin, this became *sciurus*. Later, in English, this came to be *skuyrell*, and finally *squirrel*.

Most squirrels—though not all—live in trees. Tree squirrels that live in the United

Treetops provide a safe haven for squirrels.

Red squirrel (left) — the smallest U.S. squirrel

Fox squirrel (right) — the largest U.S. squirrel

States are red squirrels, gray squirrels, and fox squirrels. In spite of their names, the main difference is not in color but in size.

Red squirrels are the smallest of the three, about 7 inches long with a 5-inch tail. They weigh about ½ pound. They live mostly in forests, often in mountain areas. They have a white ring around the eyes, and in winter they grow little tufts of hair called "ear plumes" that stick up from the ears. They

12

are usually foxy red in color, but become more brownish in winter. One species found in the northwest is sometimes called the *chickaree*.

The *fox squirrel* is the largest squirrel in the United States. It's about 15 inches long, with a tail of about 13 inches. It usually weighs about 2 pounds, although one jumbo fox squirrel was found that weighed 3½ pounds. Fox squirrels are found in forests in the south. They often live near swamps. Most fox squirrels are gray, but once in a while you may see one that is all black, except for a white nose and white toes.

But it's the *gray squirrel* that's probably best known, the one you see frisking about in city parks and in suburban backyards, leaping onto bird feeders and scampering along fences.

The gray squirrel is about 9 inches long,

with a tail of 7 inches or so. It usually weighs about a pound. Its hairs are a mix of brown, black, and white, which, when seen all together, give it a grayish look. Gray squirrels are found throughout the eastern half of the United States as well as in a few small areas in the west.

In spite of their name, "gray squirrels" are not always gray. Some are jet black. These are called *melanistic*. There are groups of melanistic squirrels here and there in Pennsylvania, Michigan, Indiana, Ohio, Minnesota, New Jersey, Vermont, Virginia, and New York.

There are also white, or *albino*, gray squirrels. These are rare. But in Olney, Illinois, there are more than 1,000 white squirrels. The people of Olney are proud of these special squirrels and have laws to protect them. It is against the law to shoot them. A white squirrel crossing the street has the right of way in traffic. And anyone caught trying to sneak one out of town is fined $25. Olney is called "The Home of the White Squirrels."

Albino squirrels have also been seen in Connecticut, Massachusetts, Wisconsin, Maryland, Indiana, West Virginia, Arkansas, Alabama, and the Carolinas.

Albino (white) squirrel in Olney, Illinois

Chapter 2
How Do Squirrels Protect Themselves?

On the ground a tree squirrel seems like a timid little thing. It moves along in hopping steps. It never goes far from a tree. That's its escape hatch. At the first hint of danger, it can turn on a dime and make a dash for it. In a few seconds it's up the tree.

There it suddenly turns into a daredevil, leaping from one shaky branch to another, or hanging upside down by its toes.

But squirrels don't spend the whole day running and climbing and leaping. They do take some time off.

In winter when the trees are bare, you may see, high in a tree, a big ball made of twigs, sticks, and bark. It's built by squirrels. It's called a *feeding platform*. It's a place

16

Feeding platform

where squirrels go to rest for a while, or to eat. It's waterproof. It's comfortable. The opening is near the tree trunk. Once inside, they close the "door" with twigs and grass.

Sometimes they sleep here, too. But more often a squirrel's real home, or den, is in a nest hole in a hollow tree. This is a safer place. The entrance must be not too big, but not too small. It has to be just big enough for the squirrel to get in and out, but not big enough for an enemy to fit in.

Look at a squirrel face, close up. See the long whiskers? There are five rows of them. And they are almost 3 inches long. These are used as space-fitting guides. They stick out about as wide as the body. They keep a squirrel from wedging itself into a hole that's too tight to get out of. (If there is not

A young squirrel's face, close up

enough room for the guide hairs, the squirrel knows the space is too small for its body.) It also has guide hairs on its paws and back.

Look at the squirrel's big bulgy eyes. Squirrels have keen eyesight. And with the way the eyes are placed, a squirrel has good "wide-angle" vision. It can look way off to the side, and even look up or back without

Bulgy eyes help squirrels spot their enemies.

moving its head. The eyes are fast focusing, too. This is very important for a small animal whose best defense is to spot an enemy soon enough to be able to make a quick getaway.

Squirrels have a lot of enemies. Hawks. Owls. Raccoons. Weasels. Fishers. Foxes. Skunks. Snakes. Snapping turtles. Cats. And human hunters. Sometimes a squirrel is even found inside a big fish.

This is why squirrels are so at home in city parks. There they have trees and food, but very few enemies.

When the United States was first settled, the pioneers shot so many squirrels that their rifles were called "squirrel guns." People ate squirrel stew, squirrel pie, and squirrel dumplings. Some people still do. Today more than 25 million squirrels are shot by squirrel hunters every year.

With all these enemies, how can squirrels

survive? They manage. They're not big or powerful. But they're nimble and fast. So for self-defense they depend on fast danger-detection, and a fast getaway.

In short bursts, squirrels can run 15 miles per hour. And they never let themselves get too far from a safe haven—a tree. When there's snow on the ground, you can see that squirrel tracks don't take the shortest direct path. They go zigzag, from tree to tree.

Squirrels never go too far from a tree.

A squirrel can be up a tree in seconds. If you go close to the tree trunk and circle around it, the squirrel may see you as a threat. As you circle around, the squirrel will do the same, always moving fast, around to the opposite side of the tree. You probably won't see the squirrel anymore. It can circle faster than you can. Finally it will disappear among the leaves or pop into a nest hole.

The squirrel's sharp claws dig into the trunk.

If a squirrel spots an enemy close by—a hawk, for example—and can't get to the safety of a nest hole fast enough, the squirrel has another life-saving trick. It will flatten itself out on the trunk of the tree and "freeze," motionless. Blending against the bark, it is hard to see. Maybe—it hopes—it will be overlooked.

How can a squirrel be so surefooted as it dashes up and down 50-foot-high trees? Look at the long, sharp claws. They dig into the trunk and keep the squirrel from falling (the way rock climbers use pitons to hook onto the ice or rock).

Running down, it goes fast, headfirst, the sharp, long claws digging into the trunk. They grab onto rough bark better than smooth bark. Sometimes you can see little parallel lines on a tree. These are "slip marks," showing where the toes slipped a bit before the claws could dig in.

Chapter 3
All Kinds of Food to Feast On

In spring and summer, there's plenty of good food for squirrels. They nibble on fresh tree buds and new grass. They eat snails and caterpillars, and all kinds of insects. If there are maple trees around, they will scratch under the bark to get to the sweet sap. They love berries, cherries, apples, and corn.

Squirrels are busy in summer. They weave together twigs and branches and shredded bark to build new feeding platforms. And they repair the old ones, too. If feeding platforms are not kept in good

A gray squirrel (opposite) gnaws on a nut.

repair, they fall apart very quickly.

Pinecones are another popular food. Squirrels rip off the stiff outer scales, then lick up the seeds inside. But most of all they eat nuts—all kinds of nuts.

You and I need a nutcracker to open nuts. Squirrels use their teeth. Their front teeth (*incisors*) are long and sharp. Holding the nut in their fingers, they steady it with their upper incisors and bite up through the shell with their lowers. Then, with the lower

A black (melanistic) squirrel holding a nut

incisors (which are longer than the uppers), they pick out the nut meat. All this takes only a few seconds.

Incisors keep growing throughout the squirrel's life. They grow 6 inches a year. But they don't keep getting bigger and bigger because they get worn down as they're used. You might see a squirrel that looks like it's smiling. It's not. It's grinding down its teeth.

If a squirrel is sick, or for some reason stops gnawing on hard stuff, then the teeth grow longer and longer. This is bad news for the squirrel. The upper teeth, as they grow, curve inward, then up. Finally they can pierce the roof of the mouth, and the squirrel will die.

One day, in late summer, passing a big tree in a park near where I live, I saw a squirrel hanging, head down, his body pressed flat against the tree trunk. In this position, he looked very long and thin. He was eating something, holding it in his front paws. His back legs were spread out, with the claws gripping the trunk, holding him up. As he hung there, casually eating, he seemed to be defying gravity.

The ground all around was littered with pieces of prickly nuts of some sort. I bent down to pick one up. A second later the squirrel was gone. I looked up in the tree. I couldn't find him. But things kept falling down from above. He was continuing his eating—but in a higher, safer place.

Summer, with its feast of different foods, doesn't last forever. Tree squirrels as a rule do not *hibernate* (go into a deep sleep as a way to pass the winter) as some animals do. Instead, in the autumn, they prepare a food supply for the months ahead.

Gray squirrels, using their forefeet, dig little holes in the ground and bury nuts and acorns all over the place. They take each nut, press it into a hole, cover it with soil, pack it down, then cover the spot with leaves. They repeat the job over and over.

They also stash away nuts and seeds and mushrooms in old birds' nests, among tree roots, and in tree holes.

Red squirrels living in pine forests con-

Gray squirrel using forefeet to dig
a hole and bury a nut

centrate more on pinecones. Their saving method is different. They do not usually bury things here, there, and everywhere. Instead, they collect them all in one big *cache*. They drag 150 pinecones or more, one by one, to a nice damp spot, near a stream or under a rotted log. (The dampness keeps the pinecones from drying out.)

As winter approaches, squirrel hair grows long and thick. Even their whiskers get longer. Under their skin a layer of fat is formed. Under their outer hairs they grow a thick woolly undercoat. Even the soles of their feet get furry.

In winter, tree squirrels hole up in a nest hole, high in a tree. It's safe. It's warm. Sometimes eight or nine will snuggle in

In winter (opposite), squirrel hair grows long and thick.

together. They wrap their tails around themselves like a blanket.

When it's really cold, say zero degrees Fahrenheit, you don't see many squirrels around. In big rainstorms—winter or summer—they stay put, too. They do not like to go out when there's mist or fog either. In weather like that, it's harder for them to see an enemy in time.

But when it's not rainy or snowing or foggy or super cold, they do come out. They are most active in early morning and late afternoon. You can see them, nose to the ground, hunting for buried nuts.

How can a squirrel remember, months later, where he (or she) buried all those nuts? He *doesn't* remember. He finds them by smell. So the nuts a squirrel finds may not be the ones he himself buried. Most likely they were buried by some other

How can a squirrel remember
where it buried all those nuts?

squirrels. It doesn't matter. He finds theirs.
They find his. It's like a community food
supply. It all evens out in the end.

Squirrels are certainly not lazy when it
comes to getting something to eat. In the
Sierra Nevada mountain range in Califor-
nia, the small red squirrels called chickarees
sometimes burrow through 10 feet of snow
to get to their food.

What happens to the nuts and acorns

that are buried and nobody finds? They're not wasted. A lot of nut trees and oak trees sprout up in unexpected places. They grow from nuts and acorns buried by squirrels. (Nuts are a form of seed. Acorns are the seed of an oak tree.) So some of the trees we see have been "planted" by squirrels.

Most squirrels don't seem to drink much water. At least you don't see them doing it too often. There is water in the food they eat—in berries and other fruits, and in leaves. They also may drink all they need up in trees, from water collected in "saucers" made by tree limbs. In winter you might see a squirrel eating snow. Once, on a very cold day in the park, I saw two squirrels sucking on pieces of ice they had scratched off from a frozen puddle.

They don't like having water on their fur. When a squirrel does drink, it wipes off its chin on the ground or on a branch. If their feet get wet, squirrels lick them dry. And when they get out from swimming, they shake themselves off, the way dogs do.

They're good swimmers. One squirrel watcher in North Carolina saw a squirrel swim across a reservoir ¼ mile wide. (This is the equivalent of 8 laps in an Olympic-size swimming pool.)

Squirrels do a sort of dog paddle, with head above water and the tail stretched out partly above water. Air gets trapped in the bushy tail fur, so it acts as a flotation device to help keep the squirrel buoyant.

Chapter 4
Some Puzzling Squirrel Habits

Sometimes you might see squirrels eating soil. Why do they do that? One theory is that soil contains some vitamin that they need. But no one is sure.

Sometimes you can see squirrels taking dust baths. They roll around in dust and sand. They probably do this to get lice out of their fur.

One day a woman in North Carolina saw a squirrel in her backyard doing some really strange things. First it dug a little bit. Then it pushed its face into the earth, rolled around, and suddenly started to leap up, turning somersaults in the air. It did this over and over.

The squirrel came back every day for a few days and continued this routine. Not only did it keep coming back but it growled and stamped and chased away any other squirrels who came close.

The woman tried to figure out what was going on. When she looked at the spot carefully, she saw it was filled with ants.

Birds sometimes do something called "anting." They roll around on ant hills. Scientists think they may do this to rid their feathers of lice. (Ants squirt out an acid that kills lice.)

Was the squirrel "anting"? It seems like a possibility.

Some years an unusual squirrel event occurs. All at once squirrels—millions of them—will leave a particular area. First they seem restless. Then, suddenly, they're on the move. They all travel in the same direction. Once they get going, nothing stops them. This is called a *mass migration.*

In the autumn of 1964, millions of squirrels in Georgia began a mass migration from north to south. As they traveled, they paid no attention to anything in their path. One squirrel, swimming across the Allatoona Reservoir, found a rowboat in front of him. He didn't change his direction. He just ran up an oar, jumped into the boat, ran across the shoulders of the man who was rowing, jumped back into the water on the other side, and continued swimming south!

In 1968 the squirrels were again on the move in many Eastern states—Alabama, Georgia, Kentucky, the Carolinas, Virginia, Pennsylvania, and New York. Possibly 20 million squirrels were involved, in an area covering hundreds of thousands of miles.

While on the move, squirrels are no longer cautious and wary. They become fearless to a foolish extent, and seem to pay no attention to danger. During the migration in 1968 the number of squirrels killed on the roads was 1,000 times more than normal!

In New York State, 50 tons of drowned squirrels had to be pulled out of one reservoir. (That's about 100,000 squirrels.) It's not that they can't swim. They probably dived in when they were already exhausted, and just couldn't make it across.

What causes these mass migrations?

Sometimes the reason seems to be food shortage—not enough nuts and acorns that year. But this is not always true. Sometimes the squirrels start out looking well-fed and in good shape.

Another reason might be overpopulation—just too many squirrels in one area.

How far do the squirrels travel? Do any return? We don't really know. For a while squirrels are scarce in the area. Then, bit by bit, the population builds up again.

Chapter 5
Growing Up

Squirrels often mate twice a year—usually in January and July. The mother squirrel prepares a nest in a hollow tree. She shreds bits of bark to make the nest soft and springy. Sometimes the father squirrel helps by carrying in grass and twigs.

Six weeks later, the babies are born. There are usually two or three, although there can be as many as six. Blind and hairless, they are helpless little things. They weigh ½ ounce and are less than 2 inches long. When the mother leaves the nest for food, she covers up the babies so they are warm and safe.

They drink their mother's milk and grow fast. In two weeks, they have some hair. In four weeks, their eyes open. In five weeks, they are 5 inches long, with a 4-inch-long tail. They begin to try to sit up. Often they just flop over.

Now, when the mother comes back, they climb up inside the hollow tree trunk to greet her. They purr and sniff and touch her.

At six weeks old, they follow their mother out. First they have to get used to the light out there and all kinds of new sights and sounds.

There are different things for them to learn: how to lay down a squirrel trail (with urine), and how to follow a trail (by smell). Now they start to eat grass and other foods, though when back in the nest, they still drink their mother's milk.

In another week or so, they're almost

Young squirrels creep timidly by themselves.

ready to venture out by themselves. First they just creep up to the den entrance and peek out. Then they go out—but only a few inches from the entrance hole.

If there's any danger, they holler for their mother by making loud, high-pitched screams. If a baby falls out of the tree by accident, it makes a special kind of "lost baby" cry, and its mother rushes to help.

Finally, they really go out on their own.

Young squirrels have to learn
how to crack open nuts.

There's a lot more for them to learn. They practice burying nuts. They don't do too well at first. They don't cover the nuts properly. They have to learn how to crack them, too. First they try to crack anything around that's nut-size—even a rock. They also open nuts that are rotten or empty. But bit by bit they learn. Soon they know how to tell which nuts are good and which are rotten (by the smell). They also start to practice building nests.

Young squirrels play with pinecones, rolling them about. They dart this way and that, chase each other, and play tag and hide-and-seek. All these things help them to build up skills that will help them survive. Young that are born in the summer often stay in the same nest with their mother through the winter.

Squirrels give a short bark when alarmed. Repeating this bark a few times is a signal that warns other squirrels of danger. They also learn to pay attention to alarm calls of different birds. When in danger, squirrels may growl and snap.

They don't often have serious fights with each other. But when competing for food, or for a mate, they may fluff their tail, narrow their eyes, and sometimes take swipes at one another with their forepaws.

An older, bigger squirrel will chase off a young one if they both go for the same food.

Young female squirrels usually have babies before they are a year old. Young males must wait a bit longer to mate, because when competing for a female to mate with, the older, stronger males will chase away the younger ones.

A squirrel in the wild can live to be about seven years old. This is unusual, though. Most squirrels don't even make it through their first year. But those that do are very fit to face the threats and dangers around them.

Chapter 6
Some Unusual Squirrels

There are many kinds of tree squirrels. They live in different parts of the world.

The smallest is the *African pygmy squirrel*. Two and a half inches long, with a skinny 2-inch tail, it weighs less than an ounce. It looks more like a mouse than a squirrel. Its fur is dark greenish.

The biggest are the *giant squirrels* of Malaya and India. Twenty inches long, with a tail of about 18 inches, they can weigh 6 pounds or more. Some are deep red; some are black with yellow-striped faces. They often raid banana plantations.

There are three basic kinds of squirrels.

Giant squirrel
(above) of India

(Right) Flying
squirrels do
not really fly.

In addition to tree squirrels, there are also ground squirrels and *flying squirrels*.

"Flying squirrels" do not really fly. They glide. But they are special because they have a furry flightskin attached along each side of the body from wrist to ankle, which helps them to glide long distances.

They begin the glide with a leap, and spread the flightskin. They can control direction by the slant of the tail, and by tensing or relaxing the flightskin muscles. To slow down they raise the tail, and the body goes upright. They land on their hind legs, and grab the tree trunk with their forepaws.

Flying squirrels have long, silky fur. Their bodies are slim; their arms and legs are long.

Giant flying squirrels of Asia are almost 2 feet long, with tails even longer. Their "wingspread" is about 24 inches. Riding on air currents, they can glide along for 1/3 of a mile.

Not all flying squirrels are jumbo size. In the United States, the *southern flying squirrel* weighs just 2 ounces. The body is 5 inches long with a 5-inch tail. The *northern flying squirrel* is a bit larger. It weighs only 3 or 4 ounces.

Flying squirrels sometimes fly in groups. They are found in most parts of the United States. Still, it's not easy to get to see them. They live deep in forests, and are nocturnal, coming out only after dark.

Flying squirrels may nest in tree holes or abandoned woodpecker holes. In Asia, some nest in empty coconut shells. Giant flying squirrels build big leaf nests.

Flying squirrels are awkward and slow

on the ground, and spend practically all their time up in trees.

The third type of squirrel is the *ground squirrel*. There are lots of different kinds. They don't live in trees. Instead, they make their homes in underground burrows. Most of us have seen them, but we usually don't think of them as squirrels, because often we call them by different names.

The *chipmunk* is a form of ground squirrel. It has five stripes on its back, is about 6 inches long, and weighs only 3 or 4 ounces. Its head is large in proportion to its body. It has big cheek pouches that open into the inside of the mouth. These are used to carry food back to the den. (One chipmunk was seen stuffing 70 sunflower seeds plus 31 corn kernels into its mouth at one time.)

The chipmunk
is a kind
of squirrel.

A chipmunk lives by itself in a 3-foot-deep underground burrow. The entrance is hidden near rocks or under a log. There are separate "rooms" for food storage and sleeping, and a couple of extra emergency exits.

A young chipmunk is able to live on its own when only about two months old. The life span can be five years.

Golden-mantled ground squirrels live in the western United States. They seem to like to scurry around campsites. They are 7 to 8 inches long and weigh about 8 ounces.

The prairie dog is sometimes called the "barking squirrel."

In summer they are yellowish gold in color.

These ground squirrels chirp and buzz; when frightened, they make a birdlike whistle. Their legs are short, and their feet are big, with long, strong toes. (Some people call them *"diggers."*) Like chipmunks, they carry food in cheek pouches. The burrow they dig is small and simple: about 10 inches deep and 12 inches long.

The prairie *"dog"* is also a ground squirrel. Another name for it is "barking squirrel." Prairie dogs are found in the western United States, on the grassy prairies, where they live in large groups. They dig tunnels 12 feet deep or more. There they hollow out little separate "rooms" for sleeping and food storage. At the entrance they leave a pile of earth they use as a lookout post. One prairie dog sits up there as a lookout for danger. To see better, the lookout will bite off the tall grass nearby. If any kind of danger comes close—a coyote, a badger, a snake, or an owl—the guard barks out a warning, then ducks into the burrow. They have special "all-clear" signals. The burrow also has emergency exits.

Prairie dogs are probably the most social of squirrels. They kiss when meeting, they seem to enjoy being together, and they take turns being lookout. Sometimes thousands live together in a "town." Prairie dogs are about 12 inches long, with a short skinny tail. They weigh about 3 pounds.

Woodchuck—the largest member of the squirrel family

The *woodchuck*, or *groundhog*, is the biggest member of the squirrel family—26 inches long, plus a short tail. To prepare for winter, this ground squirrel doesn't collect food in its burrow. Instead, it collects food in its body. It eats a lot, and gets fat. In autumn, the woodchuck is at its most roly-poly: up to 16 pounds. Then it goes into its burrow and usually hibernates through the winter.

Hibernation is more than a deep sleep. The body slows down; the heart beats less, and the body temperature drops. The animal uses less energy that way. In colder climates, woodchucks go into the burrow in November and are not seen again till February or March. But those who live in warm areas can remain active all year round.

Underground, in the burrow, a woodchuck stays alone. But above ground sometimes two or three can be seen together, nibbling on clover or taking a sunbath.

Despite its fat body and short stubby legs, when in danger, a woodchuck can run 10 miles per hour for a short distance. Woodchucks are also good swimmers.

Woodchucks are found in the United States as far north as Alaska. They are also found in Canada, as well as in Europe and Asia.

The marmot is a type of ground squirrel.

The *marmot*, another ground squirrel, is closely related to the woodchuck, but smaller in size. Marmots are more social than woodchucks, and usually live in small colonies. They often live in the mountains.

Though they live on the ground, most ground squirrels are able to climb a tree to escape danger or to search for food. Like tree squirrels, they are diurnal—active in the daytime. Many, though not all, hibernate in winter. In very cold areas, some spend up to eight months of the year in hibernation. Others do not hibernate, but spend most of winter down in the burrow, coming up only from time to time. Still others, in warm parts of the world, stay active all year round.

Squirrels are in the order (group) of animals called *Rodentia*—the "gnawing mammals." The word comes from the Latin word *rodere*, meaning "to gnaw." Beavers, muskrats, gerbils, hamsters, rats, and mice are also in this order.

Tree squirrels have existed for 25 million years or more. Ground squirrels developed later—about 7 million years ago. There are now more than 1,000 different kinds of squirrels in the squirrel family *Sciuridae* (sigh-*yur*-uh-day). They are found in almost every part of the world—high in the mountains, in deserts, deep in tropical forests and on the frozen Arctic tundra.

Because present-day squirrels are not very different from the prehistoric ones, scientists sometimes consider them a "living fossil."

. Plucky and inventive, they are certainly still with us. Busily burying nuts. Leaping from tree to tree. Digging in the snow. Barking out warnings. Or casually munching on some food while hanging upside down like a trapeze artist. They seem ordinary. Yet they do some extraordinary things. And they are here and there and everywhere, making it easy for you to become a squirrel watcher.

Gray squirrel at a backyard feeder

Bibliography

Barkalow, Frederick S., Jr., and Monica Shorten. *The World of the Gray Squirrel*. New York: HarperCollins, 1973.

Godin, Alfred J. *Wild Mammals of New England*. Baltimore: The Johns Hopkins University Press, 1977.

Grzimek, Dr. H. C. Bernhard, ed. *Animal Life Encyclopedia*. New York: Van Nostrand Reinhold Company, 1975.

Natural History magazine. Letters, December 1989.

Spruch, Grace Marmor. *Such Agreeable Friends*, New York: William Morrow and Company, Inc., 1983.

Walker, Ernest P., ed. *Mammals of the World*. Baltimore: The Johns Hopkins University Press, 1975.

Webster, William, James F. Parnell, and Walter C. Biggs, Jr. *Mammals of the Carolinas, Virginia and Maryland*. Chapel Hill, North Carolina: University of North Carolina Press, 1985.

Index

Numbers in *italics* refer to photographs.